Young Scientists: Learning Basic Chemistry (Ages 9 and Up)

Speedy Publishing LLC
40 E. Main St. #1156
Newark, DE 19711
www.speedypublishing.com

CHEMISTRY is the science that deals with the structure and properties of substances and with the changes that they go through.

On the next pages are fun chemistry facts you must know...

Around 1% of the sun's mass is oxygen.

Hydrogen is the first element on the periodic table. It has an atomic number of 1.

Under normal conditions, oil and water do not mix.

Things invisible to the human eye can often be seen under UV light, which comes in handy for both scientists and detectives.

Helium is lighter than the air around us so it floats, that's why it is perfect for the balloons you get at parties.

Carbon comes in a number of different forms, these include diamond, graphite and impure forms such as coal.

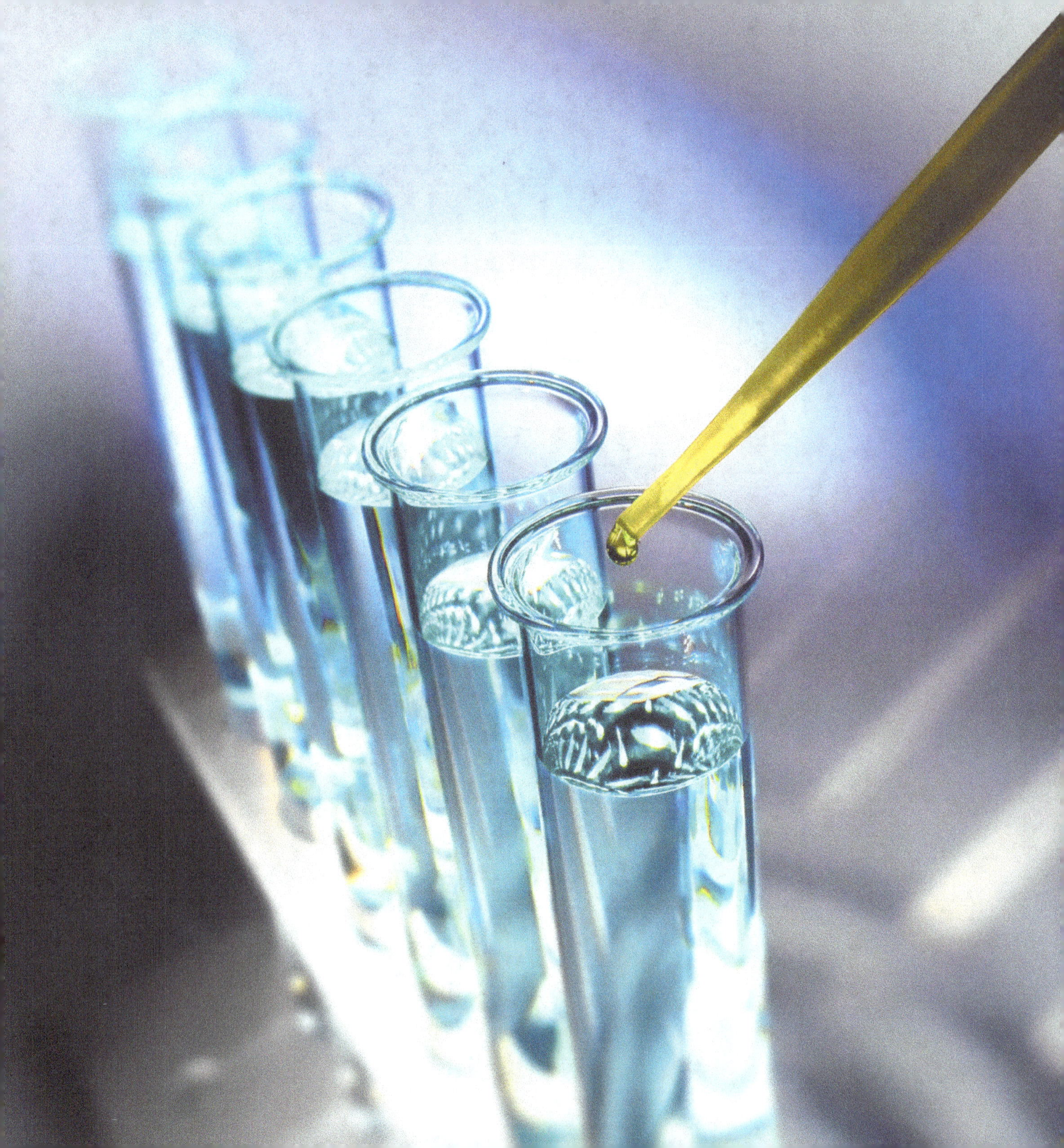

Although oxygen gas is colorless, the liquid and solid forms of oxygen are blue.

In Olympics, the caffeine in coffee is a banned substance because it can enhance performance.

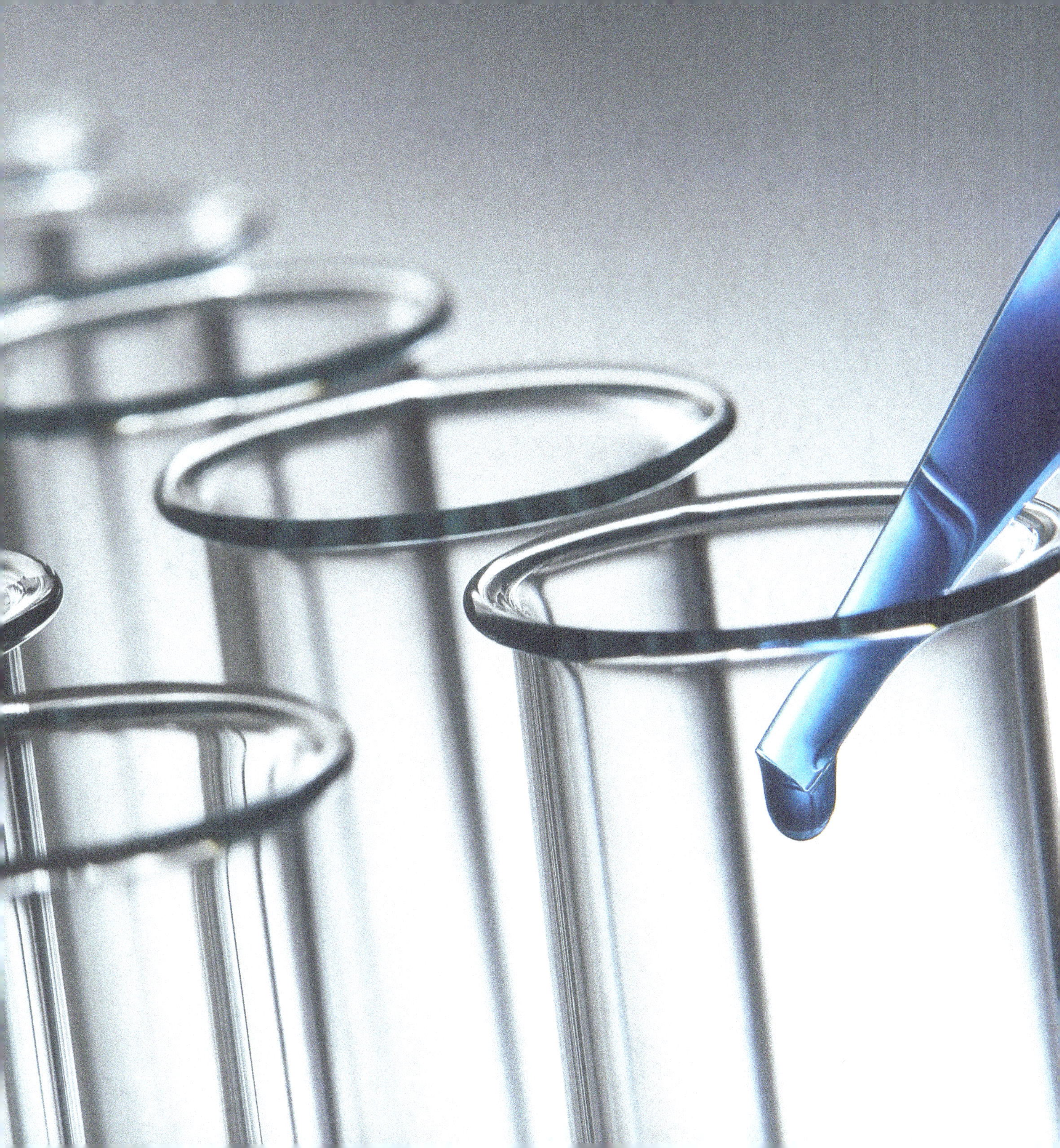

One bucket full of water contains more atoms than there are bucketfuls of water in the Atlantic ocean.

Bee stings are acidic while wasp stings are alkaline.

IN
CH 2K
50
40
30
20
10
5

Chemical reactions occur all the time, including through everyday activities such as cooking.

Humans breathe out carbon dioxide (CO2). Using energy from sunlight, plants convert carbon dioxide into food during a process called photosynthesis.

The only letter that doesn't appear on the periodic table is J.

The only two non-silvery metals are gold and copper.